skulls head samba

# skulls head samba

*poems by*
eve packer

**Fly By Night Press**
in association with
A Gathering of the Tribes
New York

COPYRIGHT ©1993 by Eve Packer
All Rights Reserved

No part of this book may be reproduced in any form without permission in writing from the publisher, except by a reviewer, who may quote brief passages in a review.

Acknowledgements: Some of these poems first appeared in *Bullhorn, Downtown, Ikon, Long Shot, National Poetry Review of the Lower East Side, Peau Sensible, Pinched Nerves, Red Tape, Verve, What Happens Next*

thanks to the Chester H. Jones Foundation National Poetry Competition, Commendation for "girl" (1993)

with enormous gratitude to the New York Foundation for the Arts (1993)

and deep thanks to Doris Packer, Steve Cannon, Matt Enger, Susan Sherman, David Trinidad, the crew of *What Happens Next* and the matrix of the l.e.s.

A GATHERING OF THE TRIBES #5—Special Edition, 1993
in association with Fly by Night Press,
P.O. Box 20693, New York, N.Y. 10009

ISBN 0-9639585-0-X
Distributed by Ubiquity Distributors, Brooklyn, New York
Printed by China Printing Company, New York

Cover and Inside Art: Thom Corn
Lay-Out & Design: Laraine Goodman & Bob Solomon
Cover Photo: Eve Sonneman
Typography: Laraine Goodman

*for sam,*
*for thom*

# contents

newsday .................................................. 11
queens ................................................... 12
sunday prologue .......................................... 14
memorial day monday ...................................... 15
and then night ........................................... 16
the guy on drums ......................................... 17
skulls head samba ........................................ 18
field of force ........................................... 20
indianapolis ............................................. 22
poem ("after the fever") ................................. 24
lesson ................................................... 25
joanne ................................................... 26
for the boys at the bar .................................. 27
capital gains ............................................ 28
coming attractions ....................................... 30
outtake .................................................. 32
to go .................................................... 33
undercover ............................................... 34
one for bimbo ............................................ 36
july is almost here ...................................... 38
passing torch ............................................ 39
sat nite sonnet .......................................... 40
jessie & agostin ......................................... 41
island ................................................... 42
september sonnet ......................................... 43
nina ..................................................... 44
ramirez .................................................. 45
girl ..................................................... 46
storming ................................................. 47
food for thought ......................................... 48
poem ("i know i have") ................................... 49
poem ("the sun is coming") ............................... 50
whitney biennial ......................................... 52
body & soul .............................................. 54
4/26:op-ed: rainy/cold & ................................. 55
blu-blu .................................................. 56
125 st: waiting for the #1 ............................... 57
spring can ............................................... 58
physics 1 ................................................ 59
pres clintons in town .................................... 60
poem ("Lord Byron was") .................................. 61
ike & tina, tina & ike ................................... 62
record heat .............................................. 64
sunshine ................................................. 65

# newsday

before the simpsons,
crown heights, gorbachev & bush,
before the coup toppled aristide, and
countless botched abortions, before
mississippi built like alabama and
more than half the western world on
black and tanbrown bodies shoved
and buried in mud, before the
ovens and dr. mengele, and all
those cliches, before mind overthrew
what matters
        there was a sliver of time like this
glimpse of light thru the mirror,
when earth met sky and
formed endless horizon, fish apes
& bouganvilla flourished, but
given two-footedness, the origin of
consciousness in the bicameral brain, opposable
thumb, what choice

but to devour the air,
shred heaven with our smarts,
bogart the transmission of the universe

## queens

I remember Candy parading endlessly
up & down the stairs at the old
WPA, she uses the noel coward method
it was explained to me:
count the steps, keep yr head up, &
dont trip over yr gown

I remember Candy

I remember Margot sitting in my living
room rocker, giving us the recipe
for brownies & homemade pussy—
take liver, saran wrap & some other
stuff—she described a friend as older
than water

I remember Margot

I remember Ethyl resplendent in yellow
tulle & spangled lace, gold stilettos,
dragon-red lips & nails, the winner of
the friday late-nite beauty pageant
at the Pyramid Club, Ethyl threw me
not a rose, but a blue cloth flower

I remember Ethyl

I remember Jorge Monsalve wearing
cabled sweaters over immaculate tights—
you in pink he sd you get lost
because you want to—but the day
before Xmas gave me an orange tin
butterfly

I remember Jorge

I remember Jorge who disappeared,
and Ethyl who slit his wrists
when AIDS got too much, and Margot
who OD'd on booze & drugs,
and Candy of cancer connected to
treatments for her transsexual operation,
Divine dead of a massive heart-attack

I remember Divine sitting backstage
in her pink peignoir, the whitest buddha
I ever saw, stocking over her hair, applying
fantastic black eyeliner fit for a tiger,
inclining her head, her crushed velvet voice,
thanking me for thanking her

## sunday prologue

if anyone wants this body, will you please:

    a. raise yr hand
    b. leave it on my machine
    c. put it in skywriting

if anyone wants this body,
they're keeping it well hidden,
if not invisible

or am i beeping the wrong signals?

## memorial day monday

in the foreign film, alien space-saga,
i look up, see the sky, burnt-out
tenements, sit on the bench,
watch the fat kid from
jersey copping smack,
walk upstairs, past the locked door,
to a treehouse,
where on the platform, on the rug,
on the floor, next to old paperbacks,
condoms scattered on jackets,
cigarettes and vodka, flesh cuts loose,
and for an hour we play hookey
from reality, joined at the hip, the fulcrum,
the hinge where space
zeroes in, bellyflopping, riding the waves,
cresting the foam, bodysurfing
all the way home, sweat pouring
down/gracing our skin/benediction,
blessing, gift

## and then night

      undulating
night, dark & phosphorescent, washes
      over this bedroom, this
bed, moving onto 3 a.m. i get up, write:

   its the hour of ncn & watermelon,
   green (apples) red (zinger tea) the hour
   when men (son, friend) nod off, cats fed, dog shit
   cleaned up, jazz, vodka, chicken
      okra rice conversation
& variations tucked in...men sleep, women stay up,
   sit at the loom of yr mind, weave in
   shade shadow shapes, the story of dark
      and light
traced on the wall, currents of cool air
   a gulf stream on yr shoulder, listen to yr hair grow,
      breathe

blue dawn coming on
 serene and sad open sea

& in the morning,
love, sweetwater

# the guy on drums

Life slowing down
to between the
lines, alligators on the
        run, hippos that
   cant
      say
         no,

               vodka
               & v-8:—and you flash on that spot you
                   keep secret, the one w/
                   the shelves & little
                   treasures—old photos,

                   places you've been to,
                   run from, gone to hide,
                   bedroom in cordoba,
                   garlic & bouganvilla,
                   getting slapped
                   upside the head
                   cause you sd
                   he reminded you of
                   billy the kid, socked

                   in the stomach, all
                   tied up, those days
                   are finished, done: dark nites
                   in dark alleys,
                   hung over, high-heeling it home,
                   paintbrushes in
                   the toilet, blood
                   down yr nose,
                   dont play that shit,

                   no slap me around, keep yr hands
                   to yrself, yr fly zipped up,
                   no more head smashed
                   up against the
                   wall, keys dropped
                   in the hallway,
                   robot dance, robot
                   ventriloquist
                   talk...

## skulls head samba

once i fought so hard
for life   stood in the
doctor's office      screamed
i have to survive—my
son and i cld feel
myself falling thru
a hole and down the chute
to the bottomless pit—
the rug a churning green
sea under wobbly knees—
my feet in sandals 'cause
the weather was warm but
at least i knew who i
was
    —thursday nite
and i take lygia barettos
afro-brazilian class     we samba
to the sekire and conga, i swim
again, bike home, pick
up pea soup, carrot juice,
jane calls from downstairs,
locked out, i let her in,
she uses my window to climb
up to her place the straw that breaks
the camel's back or is it
we won the battle but what
about the war if i have
one more responsibility, one more
disappointment, one more
night when i want
to hang out but he needs to step
off, i wont do anything—thats
the funny part, wont take straight
edge, knife, revolver, or side

of building, wont have a drink, pop
a pill, do dope, its not my
style—im far more likely
to walk into a truck—but will
skip that option, i have a
son—
    tomorrow is another day,
take care of
the body mom used
to say take care of
the body the soul
will take care of
itself—we know
better—if the soul sambas,
the body soars—

## field of force

frida's got diego inscribed, etched
on her brain, and i spose
we all have those men who
cut their way into our heart's
muscle memory—
                     the ones who catapult
into yr atmosphere,
disturb the furniture of yr
anatomy, switch the station
on yr private video, bring
up the pitch on the radio,
so yr carapace is split,
and there you are, pulsing,
alive, saying yes

## indianapolis

razor blades to the wrist
you can do yourself abrasions
to the vagina is the significant
others shtick and not the sort of
item you whip up cause
you had to take a solo
trip downstairs in the
elevator at 4 or 5 a.m.
& getting ripped apart was
probably not #1 on yr agenda—

still, yet, but—

is it rape, make that
capital R, or just the
s.o.s.—same old save our
soul shit so he hurt
you what else is new
now that youre all
grown-up, who was the
fool taught you
sex is tender, kind, smooth?

& what sense
can college make
since you apprenticed
the right woman stuff: never
mess with a man unless
you can take his heat,
hand, the totally out
spectrum of his anatomy,
mind and member
                    up under

yr skirt—when the door
clicks and the only furniture
in the room is a bed
built for two—be prepared
not for roses, moondrops,
champagne & pillowtalk—
but a whiff, tad, smidgen,
speck, just a pinch
of blood

## poem

after the fever
& the rain
brandy
blazing jazz,
behind the glass,
under ice,
pure flame
in yr face
flowers salt-sea spray

lesson

He pushes her up against the chicken wire fence
pinches her nose and theyre miles from
civilization by which she means manhattan

watching the boys in the schoolyard
play post-midnite basketball
next to mcdonalds but far from home

sitting on the curb crying from low
blood sugar and too much 100 proof
smirnoff she thinks this is the wrong

end of the telescope we know who we are
but how did we get here and how the hell
will we ever make it

back or forward to the night when
he grabbed her leg carried her into
the bedroom made sure she knew

how much a man could love her

## joanne

cant see the letters
cause the alphabet is
 all blurry

& knows she does
just terrible things
 to barbie

by the time she gets
the Halloween card
dead of AIDS
 at 6

## for the boys at the bar

how unhip
to be a jew
sad, lonely, worn

how unhip to take a straitedge
and dissect
the exact locus of pain

how unhip to be female
over the hill, alone

& how unhip to complain

## capital gains

one is lightskin
well more lightskin
than the other
& yger &
his lips are red
as if hes been
sucking on kool aid or
cherrycoke or
blood & his
shirt is hanging
raggedyandy over his pants
and hes not
walking too
well on w. 43rd
in his blue polyester
pants the other
in his white overalls
black turtleneck baseball
cap carries the aura
of sonny liston, lawrence taylor,
or howlin wolf packing iron
& he says:
you can walk
a little ahead
of me now go
inside &
sit rt down

the kid looks
like one of
those mexican marionettes
you press the wood
lever and the toy figure
jumps up and down only
somehow theyre
always getting broke, never
work quite right, so the arms &
legs are out of kilter jerk
and dangle as he turns the
corner into churchs fried
chicken halal indo pak curry
restaurant allows himself
one glance back turns
so noone can see the water
he has to wipe from under his
eyes then he can keep stepping
take his seat tho god knows
how he'll keep his ass on any chair
and the dude picks up speed stride
power his boots burn craters
in the 8th ave. cement even when hes
not angry hes furious

& bush nite before last
in his state of the union
message telling us the
cure for our woes is
a cut in capital
gains tax, whatever that is—

never let the man
see you cry, eat yr
fried chicken, split
if you can

love by any other tag:
all-out combat

29

## coming attractions

theyre falling like bowling
pins on the l.e.s.:
in may it was
grady, in
june, geezer,
then a respite
& at the end
of the holidays
khushenaton &
just when
we thought spring
was here

philip murdered,
bugsy shot to
celluloid smithereens
in the rain
we cab it home
bicker again
like the projectionist
in the booth jawing on
hubba-bubba or juicy fruit
to stay awake, keep
the film going, ignore
the body count, its

just a movie, you wanna
fold both of them
under the leaves and petals
of yr leather jacket, pajamas
if you wore them, but
keep yr mouth shut,
cry in the bathroom,
read yr nicholas freeling
sleep
& in the a.m.
get to work
on time

tues. you saw
birds flying & thought
not that scenario
again—no more phone
calls, yartzheit candles,
birds in formation heading
south or west, no more
running the credits while
the music soars please no more
roll call of the dead

## outtake

raving
into the
sunshine
I want a
real man
not
a fucking
facsimile
sipping
coke
waving her free
arm like lenny
at the podium, joy
to the world,
sacre du printemps,
rites of spring
on w. 43rd

## to go

really we'll get it all
mixed up, like a sunday brunch
special souffle, or a knock-out
mtv video where the cutting and
sounds and images are just
so you know cool and
overwhelming: the cherry
blossom petals over the dead trucker
in the gutters body, and the wine-
scented sky the night 40 patrol
cars sped down w. 4th, the
shattered glass cut with
the fires that brightened
our dinners (fried chicken or
shrimp, veggies and rice
are important) when youre watching

the hottest tv since when? the
80's, 70's—no, better:
                    the hottest
tv since kennedy was assassinated,
watts went up in flames, and all
those truly thrilling nights viewing
endless carnage and agent orange
devastate vietnam hey i say to my
son—this is yr first major
media event—so chow down, that
combo of violence and arson sure
lends spice to the meal—remember
this is yr first—but most
certainly not last taste, just the
perfect set of ingredients
to whet the appetite

## undercover

my friend hal says relationships
are difficult and the designer
in the locker room says as
she applies the letter of
the law along with her lingerie:
if hes not a great lover
kick him out

at 14th & 8th the undercover
cop saying first thing in
the morning its fucking good
friday de jesus you tell me
was the original slave
ship look it up and
i was reading about the

german police who were
sent to poland to mop
up each and every jew
and did a just about
perfect job you and
i practically come
to blows on the silent

stairway as to whos
holocaust was worse almost
waking the sleeping baby and
lady next door how terrible
we are and then we get
inside, close the door, probably
fight some more, till the light

is out, and undercover of
night (we drop the cop) and
out better selves merge
reemerge change shape color
and form shimmering hexagons
triangles circles lavender
yellow red kaleidoscope

making love means making love

## one for bimbo

we sd it
cldnt happen here
& we sd it cldnt
happen again &
when you
call—& not too
late I'm not
surprised &
then you say
Bimbo's dead:

& I'm sure its
a joke it must
be a bad joke
but i can hear
by the jack daniels
in the frayed edges
of yr voice that
its a bad joke
come true: Bimbo died
in the classroom today,

standing stage center,
broom in hand saying
to cupcakes as
the lights go down:
you sold yr soul and
this aint no market-
place...now mikey and
cupcakes and bimbo and
lord knows who else out
of short eyes is gone...

stacked like cordwood,
added to all the other
corpses accumulated this
year they make quite the
urban flesh and bone
pyramid and at the center
of the pyramid a flame (eternal),
(smoke-ash & soot-sprayed) it reads: keep
this soul trash-free, & like the kids,
sing-song in rhyme: so-&-so is

gone, he left his spirit
to carry on: lucha, lucha
la guerra es de quien
lucha y si luchas ganas—
fight, fight, war is for the fighter,
and if you fight, you win:

throw down pennies & flowers,
light one for Bimbo Rivas,
the candle
of the lower east side

## july is almost here

and we walked down the westside highway
thru the gay pride parade, so many semi-
naked bods, shorts and halters, hide-and-peek
see-thru lace tops, earrings and boots,
pink and red ribbons signifying you
know what spliced w/beer and soda pop
you can get yr paste-on tattoo right
out on the street with the condom you
find at yr feet you can walk to the
marina at battery park city and find
a divergent universe: clean and white and
beige and blue, you can sit at a table
eat a burger and/or turkey sandwich
watch the sun set orangey-pink florescent
sphere over the hudson thru the masts
of the yachts you can spot the rose and
cerulean sky catch the sapphires and
rubies strings of topaz and diamond lights
stringing the new jersey skyline you can
stand in the dentists office and read
what marlene wrote to jean: i need yr
arms, the heat of yr body—

## passing torch

shes like, no she is a tiger,
this redhead tartar fm czechoslovakia,
arizona, and her eyes are green
as glimmerglass, rainforest, tundra
brush, you know she can do anything,
cook, clean, make wonderbloom magic appear
and disappear, rabbits sprint out of hats

of the mind and heart, shes got gold and silver
tears up her sleeve, and sitting at the
table, under the nightair, breeze blowing
in from the bahamas, she passes the torch,
the courage of the cougar, the lions
guts, she cries for you—when animals
hurt she says they howl

or attack, and when theyre ready to die,
they crawl off—i was taught fight
or flight: to box you have to be carefully
trained, watch the other animals work
out, punch the bag, jump the rope,
feint and jab—or you can run—

looking at my kimono hanging on
the brick wall, purple and orange
shell-white flowers, skimming the contours
of a new world, like a sketch in invisible
ink, hinted at, but not yet
found, rubbing my leg muscles, getting
mind into shape—

no more carrying, think of him
as passing torch—

## sat nite sonnet

to me all the other nights
are up for grabs, but sat nite
you hang w/the one
you dig:
you can wok that shrimp,
catch a flick or some jazz,
sit on the stoop,
watch the stars shift
and drift thru
the spheres,
it dont make no never mind
just so

    you hang w/the one
        you dig

## jessie & agostin

shes walking
on the street
night
& shes alone
by the streetlamp

praying for a pick-up but
noones there: shes got on
a pinkpeach dress, polyester
silk-like sheath, high heels
and a walk like molasses

on wheels, and shes zonked on crack,
needs to find a trick and fast;
hes got on tight levis, t-shirt,
tattoo of an eagle, heart w/mom,
snake and angel, and he takes her up to

his room: he thinks hes in love,
and then they hear the scream:
cause this luscious vision is a boy:
theres the neighbor at the door, and

the police arrive, and they find
her body ripped, slashed, mashed
pulverized, torn: iron bar, box
cutter, screwdriver, knife, then he jumps from
the window, thats how much shame hes in:

sometimes she wore tigerskin,
always blue eyeshadow queen of the
nile, him, he was fresh
out of prison, who won, who lost,
whats the score

journey me   journey me   journey me out past
silver-pink lightning fishscale waves of sound

journey me gone

# island

    you'll think of it as light, as indigo,
maybe, or shell, sandforest or
rain mountain, river over rock, rover

    thru coral spring water, youll
think of it as panther, iguana, lizard,
parrot, garden fountain, oshuns fan, youll

    think of it as hibiscus and bouganvilla,
orange-feather laced purple-lavender
jacaranda fern-green, youll think of it

    as breadfruit, coconut, and palm, starfish
carambolla citron fresh lime-pink guava, don q
and cruzan rum, youll think of it as saltcod

    in batter, bbq chicken beans and rice mashsweet potato
and raisins, johnny cake each (5 bucks off the truck), youll
think of it as ponce slice of rose meringue sliding

    into the harbor, youll think of it as winding
road beach, twisting phosphorescent reef, youll think
of it as balcony over sea

    and sky, as film, story, scene, and
youll think of the moves, the action,
from bed to balustrade and back.

youll think of colors blue
white and dark, surf
under spine, spilling thighs

and sheets pillow solar plexus
mouths—youll think of bodies
as tide, fire and foam, crests

    & troves, ocean/light, and youll think
                  how did it happen

## september sonnet

nows the time on the machine bought
by my teen son whos not eating enuf
protein, has taken to long afternoon
naps, reading mafouz and fitzgerald,

how did it come about, while i glance
at newsday sitting on the stoop on
103rd, perusing famine in somalia,
watermelon slices bagel and tea,

now that fall is here, its back
to work and school, and the sky
a tent of heaven in blue and
lemon meringue, key lime yellow,

the water aquamarine, night
and morning woven spangled
royal purple

## nina

    oh its just one of
those passion things—
yr gizzard ripped out
again & again

i used to be my sensible self
she says

now carry skull heads in
tiny red velvet bag

# ramirez

ramirez is tough.

ramirez is from the s. bronx.

ramirez likes to parade
naked in front
of the mirror
wearing nothing
but a g-string
& rhinestone earrings

Ramirez is tough.

She teaches retarded kids reality.
how to read and write, multiply
& divide mixed fractions, find
perimeter (distance around a
closed figure). the kids lap
her up.

Ramirez is tough.

she tells her girlfriends: i dont have
a pretty face, you want
a man, go to a bar, put on
cleavage, they'll never know
the difference—

she falls in love
with a pockmarked
jewish cop from brighton
who goes back
          to the wife and kid—
men will do that—

Ramirez doesnt cry.
Doesnt put on cleavage.
Goes for a long walk.
parades in front of
the mirror—then
it swallows her—

## girl

today i visited
Shakeema whos
13 and weighs 300
lbs, has asthma
& is very black &
smart can conjugate
beber, comer, tomar, vivir,
ir, even if she cant
breathe, in an apt that's filthy & littered
w/clothes & baby books &
farina a man screaming open
the door dirty dishes and
hip-hop roaches
who cares

im outta here
(i get to go home)

## storming

you think yr dick
is worth this shit:

i got news for you:
youre nothing but
passing prick

          waiting
for a taxi w/mommy at the corner of
w 43rd & 9th, so small in
red raspberry raincoat, blue umbrella brown
eyes blinking against the rain, me thinking
one day some mans gonna stick her, burn holes
in her soul call it love, scar not vulva
or clit, but molten core—

no need to cry or bleed,
pussy Explode

## food for thought

i was going out with this
alternative lawyer: ponytail, spitfire,
honda, the works: so i got scabies from
him at his place in brooklyn, and he
denied it, the next saturday when i stepped
into the spitfire i sd did you see a
doctor, and he sd: i never go, so i sd:
well im better and im not going to brooklyn
or fucking so he checked not it but out
                              i tell didi
my story and as she leaves,
the girl sitting on the ledge
in the steam room who looks
like a naked
botticelli, recently emerged
from water, doing mysterious
things w/her hair says: i was in
a monogamous relationship and

got herpes, and he denied it,
i was in a monogamous relation-
ship and got crabs and he denied
it; the herpes was so bad they had
to freeze my cervix or i wld have
gotten (the C word)—

if only men really were pigs we cld
barbecue & convert them into
something useful and tasty—

# poem

i know i have
a cunt,
and am a cunt;
i dont have to
fuck some new &/or yg
thing to prove

im here

## poem

the sun is coming
thru the window a morning
time you used to drink
yr coffee i turn on 89.9
and billies singing all
or nothing at all

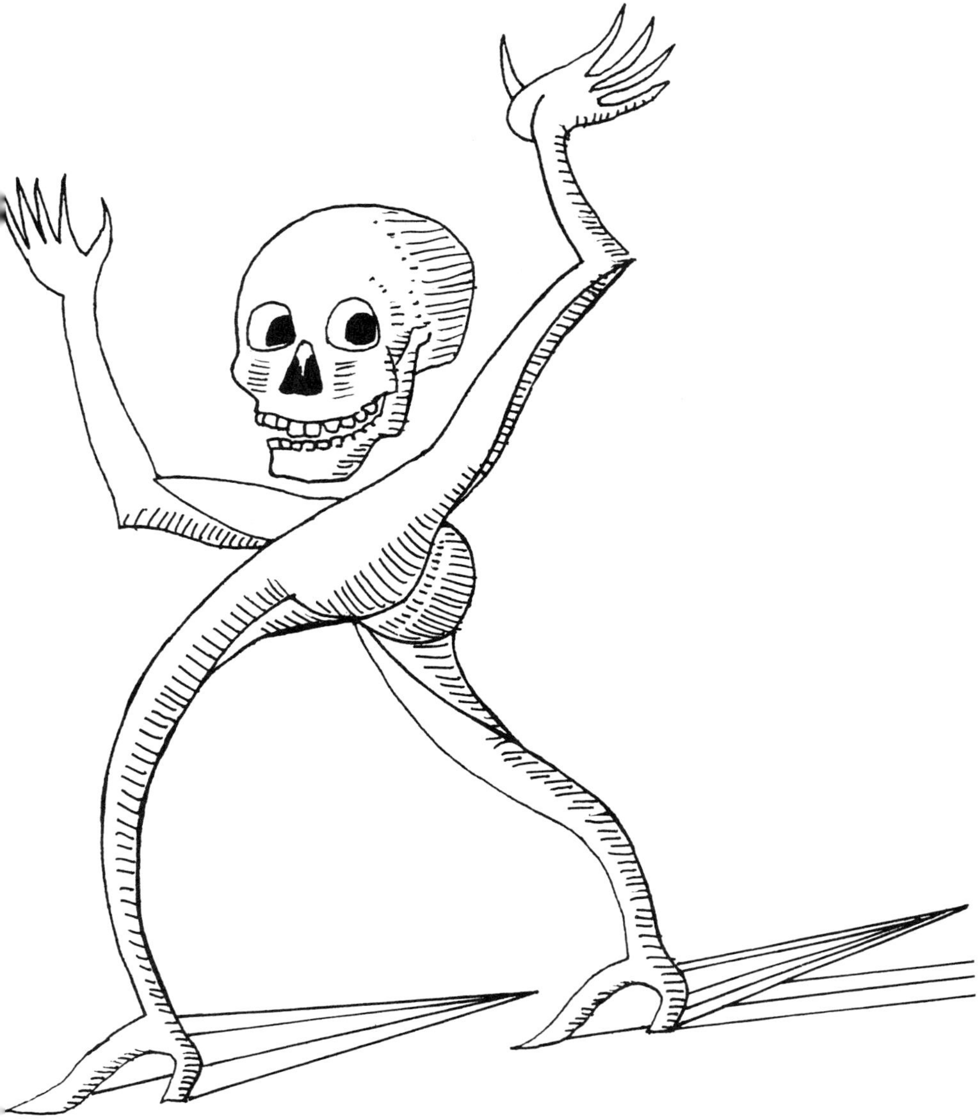

## whitney biennial

which is
sort of
like a
circus tho
less silly fun
than the
calder downstairs, or
the one a few weeks
back at thread waxing
space, & if i see
one more mapplethorpe nude
of ken moody who
works as a trainer in
my health club, which gavin
rejoined today...

but i
do like
the cindy sherman photo
of a plastic old
man face, woman
plastic tits &
fat tum, black dick
coming from
gorgeous red
painted
cunt & lots of
Dynel all
round.

and i like the sue
williams, & nancy spero
(of ana mendieta) &
the kiki smith cause
im a sucker for (or am)
a crystal tears
mother but my favorite

is a quote by a long-dead dark
dude: 'a sea-fight must either take
place tomorrow or not, but it is not
necessary that it shld take
place tomorrow, nor is it necessary
that it shld not take place—)
                    aristotle

my button reads: imagine

## body & soul

It was
abt mid-
way thru the
2nd set, & up til
then the tunes had
been kinda hardriving
& fast, & then josh redman started
hitting some long
slow notes, like pulling
saltwater taffy
thru a wind
tunnel, and the chairs stopped
scraping, and the chit-chat, and
hands froze mid-air, the only
sound: heart/split

## 4/26: op-ed: rainy/cold &

tony lewis says that to deal
with a bully you have to stand up:
hes talking about serbia, and explains first

you make diplomatic appeals which you state
youll back with a show of force...then you issue
an ultimatum...)

a word that was never
entered in my pc so how cld i use it
but im paying

thru the heart;
konrad adenauer quoted in newsday today
says the only way to conciliate a tiger

is to be devoured...
it was that close, so maybe i had to use
my only bullet...

the little plastic box on my work desk
holds some tiny copper ball-bearings: yr sposed
to shake it and say: get some balls

a gift (one of the few) from you to me

## blu-blu

        blue is my
color, blue
my shade, blue-indigo-
violet the fast end of the
spectrum:
knocks you over,
so you spit
salt & sea
pray for air
get up, crack
a wave, then
fall again,
kicking, gasping,
diving til
you hit bottom
& buried
treasure, or
a shark, may-
be when
you go that
far, the shark
is the treasure,

then what?

## 125 st: waiting for the #1

Exhaustion palpable
as gold dust coats
eye, shoulderblade,
gut, a fish gutted
& worn mouth twisted
whispering for what
day w/o decisions,
a tropical storm,
stroll w/samba
afternoon sun

## spring can

i think
of all the suicide girls:
sylvia, annie,
vivien dead in
her own cough-
up stuff, cleopatra
& rene v., & leslie
& eileen who clutched
at a tree that wasnt
strong enuf—then theres
colette & the two louises (b& n),
georgia who
survived—

whats yr choice: column a
or b, the homeless
man w/dreads
says: its all what you make it

## physics 1

my city, my place, my curse, my prison,
my escape—this is my home—

>noisy today
>at 42nd & 8th
>rush hour
>running for
>the bus & train,
>tv's, ts's, whores
>& dealers
>heavy into
>it on the e
>a lady
>w/shopping
>bag beaded
>scarf contemplating
>the doppler effect—

the frequency of a wave is higher in front of a moving
object than behind it so coming toward me you might be
violet but from the back yr red

spectrum of the universe shit you step in
at the corner, they say it brings luck, and then
theres summer:


the electromagnetic field:

## pres clintons in town

a transvestite
in black lace, ripped
jeans, black flip-flops, swaying
& saying 'Oink Oink' on 8th
& 42nd—sirens pass—

for mothers day my son gave me
a bronze tortoise that had caught
my eye—
                Why? do i have a thing for turtles and
transvestites—

turtles are amphibian, slow, need
to carry a house over their back, retreat, hide,
go underwater sometimes for days—to get the guts
to come out, go soft, face the sun, get
cut—

tv's are female w/
balls & the loneliest
people i know

both wear painted glistening shield
to cover whats real

## poem

Lord Byron was
a swimmer
& he swam the
Hellespont

swore by wine & flesh
extreme measures

on yr knees in a
dungeon
candlelit dick
& mouth loving it

## ike & tina, tina & ike

at the start anna mae (later tina) is too much teeth
& smile skinny country-friendly cornflower naive
but she sure can sing

& ikes all pink sateen elvis presley sleepy
innuendo maple syrupy butter
cat & mouse paw-in-glove touch

& he puts her up front
of the band
& they hit the
road

& her tits get bigger, muscles
grow, voice stronger, her
gestures go orange-bold & sexy

& he gets smaller, wears his hair in a beetles
cut, covers up in a turtleneck, no more goofy-wolf
grin when hes working tightlip grim

but he still writes
the tunes, gets
the gigs, keeps the group
on the go

& then theres the first dressing room scene: its always
before a big show: he flips his head
& says yr voice

aint shit
& the audience gasps
cause we see the worm turn

& she tries to please him & he disses her, & she tries
to please him & he fucks whatevers in the room & disses her, she
tries to pease him & he grabs the bucks & disses her, takes
the money & goes for blow & disses her, & does more
& punches her, punches shoves pushes slaps and smacks her
around & she tries to please him & he hits her & hits
her & hits her & hits her so hard he comes & she tries
to please him & he says yr songs *nuthin'*
punches her so he almost busts her inner
tube & blood down her face she runs to
a ramada inn & after 16 yrs, steps off

before the credits they tell us that
the deeper the lotus goes into mud
the more beautiful the bud

& its true shit is the best fertilizer
but a knife to the heart is another story—
i tell my son, life is too short—

## record heat

down the stairs, to a
basement cellar dungeon
supreme, 2 candles, 1
white, 1 red (for elegua), 1
black bed, r & b radio—&
then a thunderstorm, sand & grit,
sudden squall, sugarfire, flash-
flood rain—coming up for
air—shaking off the drops—
doing a cigarette, swigging a
beer, legs spread, bonded
by sweat, heads thrown back
in victory—

sunshine

6'3"
perfect physique
form-fit t &
jeans, asking me for
30¢—for the subway—i just
got out of the hospital he says, and
flashes plastic i.d., i hand over
the change but stay away
from the plastic, i got hit
by a greyhound bus, he lifts
his shirt to show the scar (a big brown
birthmark), whats yr name i say, joey
he says, hi joey, im eve, oh eve he says,
and you can hear silk taffeta
rustle, oh eve he says, bows &
bends, hands in prayer position, oh eve im adam
can we start all over again

Eve Packer was born in the Bronx, is a graduate of the University of Michigan, attended Girton College, Cambridge, received degrees from London School of Economics and N.Y.U. She has traveled extensively in Europe and Latin America, and has taught at Queens College, the New School, and is now a Homebound Instructor. An actress for many years, then performance artist and poet, she has been awarded grants from the New York State Council on the Arts, Jerome Foundation, Puffin Foundation (w/jazz group *the Future*), and most recently from the New York Foundation for the Arts. She coordinates and co-edits the magazine for a loose collective of city poets *What Happens Next*. She lives downtown, has a son, and swims daily.